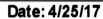

Sneakers

by Chris Jozefowicz

Content Consultant

Elizabeth Semmelhack, Senior Curator
Bata Shoe Museum

Reading Consultant

Jeanne M. Clidas, Ph.D.
Reading Specialist

Children's Press®
An Imprint of Scholastic Inc.

Table of Contents

Introduction

Everyone from professional athletes to kids at the playground wears sneakers. These shoes help people run faster, play safer, and look good.

Do you want to learn some fascinating facts about sneakers? Then read on!

This sneaker is bigger than a car

The biggest sneaker ever made is almost 21 feet (6.4 meters) long, 8 feet (2 meters) wide, and over 5 feet (1.65 meters) high.

Imagine how big a person would have to be to fit into this sneaker!

SUPERGA

Shaq is an all-around big guy. He is 7'1" tall.

Its laces are 75 feet (23 meters) long! The shoe was made in 2013 by the Italian company Superga. It was not made to wear, though. It was on display in Hong Kong, China.

Basketball stars Shaquille O'Neal (above left) and Bob Lanier hold the record for largest shoes in the NBA. Both players wore a size 22!

Some shoes had bark soles

This is an oak tree.

Modern sneakers were created in the mid-1800s. They have rubber soles. Before that, some athletic shoes had cork on the bottom! Cork comes

from oak tree bark.
It is soft and springy.
A popular cork-soled
shoe was a sand shoe.
It was used for playing
on the beach. (No one
had thought of the
flip-flop yet!)

One of the first sneakers was created for tennis. In the mid-1800s, people wore tennis shoes with rubber soles. The rubber stopped players from slipping on grass.

Can you believe this cork came from tree bark?

A waffle maker
revolutionized soles

Many shoemakers want their sneakers to have light soles. In the 1970s, Nike cofounder Bill Bowerman used a waffle iron to shape

Bill Bowerman (center) was a track coach before starting Nike.

rubber into soles. The waffle soles used less rubber, so they were light. They also had good **traction**. They didn't slip. They were perfect for running.

sap

Natural rubber comes from the rubber tree. It is made from sap. Sap is like the blood of a tree. Today, most sneakers have **synthetic**, or fake, rubber soles.

This photo shows the top and bottom of Nike's original waffle shoe.

Some sneakers stay on with air

Velcro sneakers are a good choice before you've learned to tie laces.

Some sneakers use laces to stay on your feet. Some have Velcro. Would you believe some sneakers use bags filled with air? Pump sneakers have chambers, or spaces, inside. They inflate around your foot. That way the shoes fit snugly on feet of different shapes.

Squeezing the orange pump in front makes these shoes fit just right.

Reebok made the first pump sneakers. The designer, Paul Litchfield, was inspired by ski boots. The boots had balloons inside. That helped skiers' boots stay tight. It also protected skiers' ankles.

These shoes have lots of names

Do you wear sneakers, tennis shoes, or kicks?

People have lots of names for athletic shoes. The name you use probably

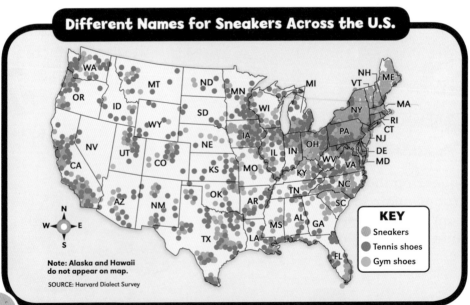

Different Names for Sneakers Across the U.S.

Note: Alaska and Hawaii do not appear on map.

SOURCE: Harvard Dialect Survey

KEY
- Sneakers
- Tennis shoes
- Gym shoes

depends on where you're from. People from the northeastern part of the United States call them sneakers. Much of the rest of the country usually calls them tennis shoes. Other names include running shoes, jogging shoes, gym shoes, trainers, and kicks.

Old-fashioned names for sneakers can tell you what people used them for. In the 1800s, some sneakers were called croquet sandals. People wore them when playing croquet. Another name was yacht shoes. A yacht is a fancy boat.

Some sneakers are not for wearing

Artist Ken Courtney made shoes fit for a king. He dunked Nike high-tops in real melted gold.

Courtney's sneakers are a work of art.

Jungen turned Air Jordans into artworks inspired by **Northwest Coast** traditional masks.

Brian Jungen is an artist who uses sneakers like other artists use clay. He cuts up sneakers and turns them into incredible designs. His sculptures are masks that often look like animals.

Courtney made five pairs of these shiny sneaks. They cost about $5,000 per pair. But even a king couldn't wear them. They were made for display only.

One person had
2,500 pairs

Jordy Geller had one of the largest sneaker collections in the world. He kept the shoes in a

Jordy Geller's collection was estimated to be worth more than a million dollars!

special warehouse called the ShoeZeum. After he built his museum, Geller decided to share his shoes. He began selling his collection in 2012.

These sneakers belong in a bank vault!

The Nike SB Dunk High-Top

FLOM is one of the most expensive sneakers ever. Only 24 pairs were made. Collectors pay more than $10,000 for a pair. The shoes are decorated with pictures of money from around the world. What does FLOM stand for? "For the Love of Money," of course!

"Smart" sneakers have brains

Some sneakers have **microchips** in them. Microchips are small parts that help computers work. In shoes they can keep track of how you move.

Puma was one of the first companies to "hook up" its sneakers to computers. The Puma RS Computer Shoe came out in 1986.

They can count how many steps you take. They can compute how far you run.

The Nike+ is a modern computerized shoe. That little red oval is its "brain."

Kids take between 10,000 and 16,000 steps every day. That adds up to more than an hour spent walking. It also equals more than 5 miles (8 kilometers)!

The U.S. has more sneakers than people

In 2014, about 320 million people were living in the United States. Those people bought more than 390 million pairs of athletic shoes. They spent

Do you have more than one pair of sneakers?

A worker shovels Nike grind onto a football field in Maine.

$21 billion on them! How many pairs of sneakers do you and your family have? What do you do with old ones when you get a new pair?

Making new sneakers and getting rid of old ones creates a lot of garbage. Nike recycles old shoes. The company grinds up the sneakers to make a mixture called Nike grind. It is used to make playgrounds and sports fields.

One day sneakers will be printed for you

These sneakers were made on a 3-D printer.

In the future, you may have your very own unique pair of sneakers. They will be designed by computers

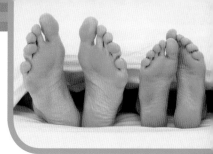

and built by a 3-D printer. The computer will take pictures of your foot. Then the printer will build up layers of plastic. This will make a shoe just for you!

This is a 3-D printer that prints sneakers.

The two shoes you are wearing are probably the same size. But your feet are probably not! Most people's feet are **asymmetrical**. That means they are not the same shape or length. Some people's feet are so different that they have to wear shoes of two different sizes!

Activity
Crazy Laces

There are many cool ways to lace a sneaker. Here's a fun style to try on your own kicks.

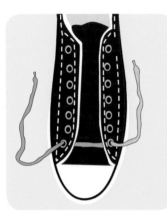

1 Run a lace straight through the bottom eyelets under the flaps, just as you would normally lace your shoes. You should have an end of lace going to the right and an end going to the left.

2 Make sure the length is even on both sides. While you hold one lace straight up, wrap the other lace around it once. This will put a loop in the laces.

3 Bring the laces back down and thread the end of each through the underside of the next eyelet.

4 Bring the ends up again and wrap one around the other. Thread through the underside of the next eyelet. Repeat until you reach the top.

When you're done, you should have laces that loop back on each other from the bottom to the top of the shoe.

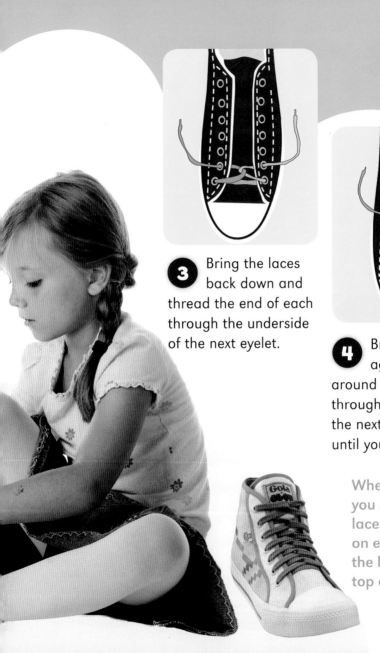

Vulcanized rubber is invented. It is tough and lasts a long time.

Basketball is invented.

1839 **1850s** **1891** **1917**

Sneakers are invented.

Converse introduces All Star basketball shoes. These are the first to have a sports star, coach Chuck Taylor, endorse them.

New laws say people will work eight hours per day, five days per week. Now there is more time for sports and play.

Velcro is invented.

| 1937 | 1948 | 1972 | 1985 | 2014 |

The shoe company Nike is formed.

The first Air Jordan sneakers from Nike create a stir. They are popular in fashion and athletics.

Americans spend $21 billion on sneakers.

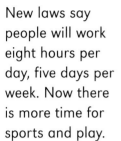

Glossary

- **asymmetrical** (ay-si-MEH-tri-kuhl): not the same on one half as on the other

- **microchips** (MYE-kroh-chips): thin pieces of silicon that contain electronic circuits, used in computers and other electronics

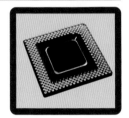

- **synthetic** (sin-THEH-tik) manufactured or artificial, rather than found in nature

- **traction** (TRAK-shuhn): force that keeps a moving body from slipping on a surface

Index

About the Author

Chris Jozefowicz began his career as a scientist before switching to writing. He is a former Weekly Reader editor and has written about wide-ranging topics for a variety of publications for children and adults. Chris's favorite sneaker invention is the little tab for the laces that keeps the tongue from sliding to the side. He lives in Louisville, KY, with his family.

Facts for Now

Visit this Scholastic Web site for
more information on sneakers:
www.factsfornow.scholastic.com
Enter the keyword **Sneakers**

Library of Congress Cataloging-in-Publication Data

Names: Jozefowicz, Chris.

Title: 10 fascinating facts about sneakers / by Chris Jozefowicz.

Other titles: Ten fascinating facts about sneakers

Description: New York : Children's Press, an imprint of Scholastic Inc., [2017] | Series: Rookie star | Includes index.

Identifiers: LCCN 2016003493 | ISBN 9780531228173 (library binding) | ISBN 9780531229422 (pbk.)

Subjects: LCSH: Sneakers—Juvenile literature.

Classification: LCC GV749.S64 J69 2017 | DDC 685/.31—dc23

LC record available at http://lccn.loc.gov/2016003493

Produced by Spooky Cheetah Press

Design by Judith Christ-Lafond

© 2017 by Scholastic Inc.

Photographs ©: cover: tatyana_tomsickova/Thinkstock; cover background: stock09/Shutterstock, Inc.; back cover, 2: Olha Ukhal/Shutterstock, Inc.; 3 left: pat138241/Thinkstock; 3 right: 20fifteen/Thinkstock; 4-5 top: jonathan_kay/Thinkstock; 4-5 background: BsWei/Shutterstock, Inc.; 5 bottom: Roman_Gorielov/Thinkstock; 6-7 bottom: Electric sekki; 7 top: David Maxwell/Newscom; 8 left: marilyn barbone/Shutterstock, Inc.; 8 right-9 bottom left: Toni Tejon/Shutterstock, Inc.; 9 bottom right: Brian Jackson/Fotolia; 9 top: Popperfoto/Getty Images; 10: AP Images; 11 top: noppharat/Fotolia; 11 bottom: Kirby Lee/Getty Images; 12 left: kdshutterman/Fotolia; 12 right: Eric Isselée/Fotolia; 13 left: Jerritt Clark/Getty Images; 13 right: rcaucino/Fotolia; 15: Glenda Powers/Fotolia; 16 frame: Picsfive/Shutterstock, Inc.; 16 inside frame background: kotoffei/Shutterstock, Inc.; 16 sneakers: JP5/Newscom; 16 background: Iraidka/Shutterstock, Inc.; 16 boy: Luis Molinero/Shutterstock, Inc.; 17 left: Sarah L. Voisin/Getty Images; 17 right: Frank Leonhardt/Newscom; 18: Howard Lipin/Zuma Press; 19 top: Flight Club; 19 bottom: Maksym Yemelyanov/Fotolia; 20: PUMA; 21 top: SerrNovik/Thinkstock; 21 bottom: Sergio Azenha/Alamy Images; 22 left: Maxim Zarya/Thinkstock; 22 right: Sergey Novikov/Shutterstock, Inc.; 23: Gordon Chibroski/Portland Press Herald via Getty Images; 24 background: Carlos Caetano/Shutterstock, Inc.; 24: Recreus and FilaFlex 25 top: Wavebreakmedia Ltd/Thinkstock; 25 bottom: Olly Curtis/MacFormat Magazine via Getty Images; 27 left: McIninch/Thinkstock; 27 right: Gola; 28 top: Ty Allison/Getty Images; 28 bottom: Northampton Museums & Art Gallery/Newscom; 29 top: danielsbfoto/Fotolia; 29 bottom: David Zalubowski/AP Images; 30 top: Wavebreakmedia Ltd/Thinkstock; 30 center top: Jan Skwara/Dreamstime; 30 center bottom: jonathan_kay/Thinkstock; 30 bottom: SerrNovik/Thinkstock.

Map by Jim McMahon

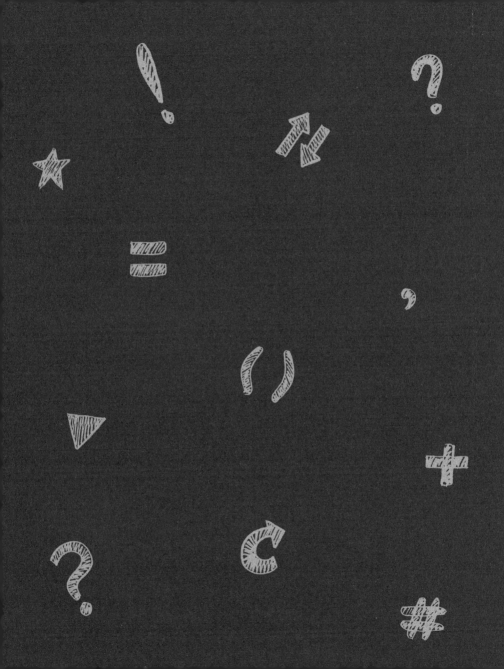